Help, God!
I'm A Pastor's Wife!

Karyl Gaehring

Acknowledgments

I would like to express my deepest, heart-felt thanks to my husband, Paul, who has been a great source of inspiration and support throughout our years of ministry together. He has recognized the gifts that God has instilled within me and consistently encouraged me while propelling me forward in the calling he saw on my life. I am proud to not only call him my husband, but also my best friend. Not only does he wear the title Father to our two sons and Grand Dad to our grand child; but he is the great example of a true Man of God. He is an incredible minister of the Word and known to so many as Dr. Paul.

Thanks to our sons, Paul and Michael, who enjoyed and survived the life of a PK (preacher's kid). Despite all odds, they have each taken up the mantle in ministry and have truly made us proud.

Thanks to my special and *best* friends, Nicole, Carol, Louise and Elsie, who have been loyal in the good times and the bad times; who are supportive when others turn their backs; and who have loved me in spite of my faults and failures. They have shared in my victories and I say to them, "Thank you for your love, loyalty, and commitment."

I pray as you read this book, that you will find it to be a source of inspiration to all women in ministry and "Pastors' Wives."

Contents

Introduction...ix

1. The Call of the Pastor's Wife............... 11
2. The Many Hats of The Pastor's Wife ... 21
3. You've Got to Roll with the Punches 29
4. Lighten Up.. 43
5. The Pastor's Home 55
6. Family Matters...................................... 63
7. Sheep Bites and Bandages................... 75
8. Spiritual Leaches.................................. 87
9. Hello… I Have My *Own* Identity 97
10. Friends 105
11. Watch Out for Jezzie Belle.................. 111
12. Don't Be a People Pleaser 117
13. Keep Your Eyes on the Prize 127

Introduction

This book is written and dedicated to all women, and those known as, the "Pastor's Wife;" who is active in ministry today, whose ministry preparation did not completely prepare them for this occupation, nor did they have any concept of the requirements that would be "expected" by the people in their congregation. Being in the ministry is truly a high calling that carries great responsibilities along with unique blessings and challenges.

Help God! I'm a Pastor's Wife is a book that many women in ministry and pastors' wives will be able to relate to. The wife of a pastor seems to always have her share of unique issues and funny stories. While not intending to take from anyone's uniqueness, this book was written to merely encourage the pastor's wife that could use some encouragement; to offer guidance to those that need some direction and support; and to embrace the Woman of God who many times feels isolated as though she's walking a very lonely road. This book is to let you know, that *you* are not alone.

"For many are called, but few are chosen."
-Matthew 22:14 (NKJV)

Chapter One

The Call of
the Pastor's Wife

The New King James Version says, "For many are *called,* but few are chosen." There is a special love and appreciation for the pastors and their wives who are indeed called and chosen into the ministry today. Blessed are they that exemplify their calling with Godly lives, lifestyles, and families. For their fruit is known by proven and anointed ministries. Never before in the history of mankind has our nation been so blessed to have so many powerful men and women of God.

It is astounding the assortment of churches today, ranging from store front, to mega church, or traditional to contemporary. Each church has its own vision and format, while being unique in their separate identity. There has never been a greater array of facilities and ministry personalities to choose from.

On the flip side of the coin, given the many religions that are in our world today, it only stands to reason that there are *some* self-proclaimed pastors, looking for what they would consider an *easy* way to *make a living.* After all, to those who have never been involved in ministry and have no concept of how a church and ministry operates, to them it appears that you can: set your own hours, be your own boss, prepare a sermon, visit a church member in the hospital, do a few weddings and funerals; then at the end of the day, lay back and enjoy life, right? No wonder the Bible says, *"few"* are *"chosen."*

In this day and hour, one had better know that they are truly called and chosen by God for ministry or they will not be able to stand in this field.

Years ago, being in the vocation of the clergy was a highly respected position that held great honor. However, in today's society, the enemy has used financial scams and moral failures among the clergy to birth disgrace in the eyes of the public. This, in turn, has weakened the fiber of trust toward the clergy of our nation.

As a result, throughout many years, it has become a challenge to be a pastor, much less the *wife* of one.

I've heard of numerous instances when a pastor married his sweetheart. Like any other couple, they planned to live happily ever after; only to find that his mate was not prepared for the unexpected pressures of being a "Pastor's Wife." Devastated and broken, she left him literally at the altar. Completely unaware of the damage that she had left behind, laid the pieces of a broken-hearted husband and a devastated church.

There aren't any schools or training that can even begin to prepare you for the "life of a pastor's wife." There is no way to prepare you for the blessings as well as assaults that tend to find you as you serve in the ministry day in and day out.

"So then, how can a woman prepare herself for the unexpected?" you might ask. "And how can anyone go into something blinded, not knowing how to prepare for what lies ahead?" Unfortunately, there is no way of knowing or predicting what will transpire in the future of a pastor's wife. With each day, within each church, or ministry, lies its own challenges and issues to overcome, along with many blessings and surprises with God on your side.

Some women in ministry today are *somewhat* prepared for the ministry from their childhood experiences of being raised in a pastor's home. Yet, many women still have no clue what they are soon to be walking in to.

In the early years of our ministry I leaned heavily on the strength of my husband. Many times people would come to me and ask Bible related questions that I was unaware of the answers. I would always refer them to my husband; however, I quickly learned that I needed to develop my *own* personal relationship with God. God was teaching me that I should not always push people off on my husband, but that He wanted to use *me* as well to provide them with their answers.

In order to become a strong woman of God, you must develop your own personal walk with Him. This takes discipline, determination, consistency, and time. You have to want God for yourself. As you spend consistent quality time with God you will develop your walk throughout your journey. During this development stage you will learn there are many levels of spiritual maturity.

In September of 1979, I woke up one morning thinking, *I need to get consistent in my own walk with God.* I wondered how I was going to accomplish that as I had two small children at the time. One son was twenty months old and the other three months old. Everyone knows how time consuming and demanding a mother's life is when her children are this small. Yet I was **determined** to know God deeper for myself.

Deciding to yield to my notion, I rummaged around and found a spiral notebook, a pen, and my Bible. My husband will be the first to tell you that I am not a morning person; but I knew if I was going to get some "alone time" with God, I would have to rise rather early before my babies would wake.

I set the alarm clock in the hallway for 5:20am. I informed myself the night before, "When that alarm goes off, you CANNOT turn around and get back in the bed! Turn it off, and keep going.

You are going to have coffee with Jesus in the morning."

Sometimes, my time with the Lord would last for hours. Once the babies were awake, I would then tend to them. Nevertheless, once they were preoccupied, either watching *Sesame Street* or napping, I proceeded to dive back into my Bible and notebook yet again.

On my very first day of journaling, I wrote, "God, I feel like you are telling me to write things down in a notebook." As I opened my Bible, this particular verse literally seemed to leap off the paper; "The word that came to Jeremiah from the LORD, saying, Thus speaks the LORD God of Israel, saying: 'Write in a book for yourself all the words that I have spoken to you'" (Jer. 30:2, NKJV).

As I sat in amazement, I could not believe what just happened! I felt like God was talking right to *me, Himself!* From that moment on, I began a thirty-year love walk that has taught me immeasurably throughout my life.

A few traits that have come out of this journey are: stability, accountability, maturity, dependability, reliability, and most of all, commitment to

God. I have learned that every thing I am questioning of, He has the answer to.

I eventually found myself falling in love with God. The more time I spent with Him, the more time I *wanted* to spend with Him. Then He led me to Jeremiah 33:3, "Call to Me and I will answer you, and show you great and mighty things, which you do not know" (NKJV). I was so excited! God was talking to *me... again*! Shortly afterwards He taught me: *"But seek ye first the kingdom of God, and his righteousness; and all these things shall be added unto you" (Matthew 6:33 NKJV).*

My time with God had become essential during this time of my life. With the challenges of having small children, of course, the enemy would try to disrupt my quiet time; but I became increasingly determined to get my time alone with the Lord. I *had* to have it and still do to this day! This time is not essentially a "have to" time; meaning God does not force anything on us, but it is nonetheless my "want to" time. I have found that my whole day flows so much better when I start it off first thing with the Lord.

Journaling has helped me to be consistent. It also has helped me to grow and mature. I have watched even my *own* progress. I now have a trunk full of journals.

The challenges and attacks and the challenges of pastors' wives today are horrendous. As I stated previously, without having a personal walk and relationship with God, it will make it most difficult, if not impossible, to set a Godly example for others, much less remain sane. Your walk with God should never become an obligation, but a saturation of a *love walk* with you and your God.

Your time with God will become a necessity if you view it as spending time with your best friend. He will become *everything* to you. Your desire will increase. Your dependency on Him will become a must. You will see and experience such beautiful things as your relationship develops with Him. He truly does have secrets stored up for those who seek Him. I love the secrets!

"A man's gift makes room for him, and brings him before great men"
-Proverbs 18:16 (NKJV)

Chapter Two

The Many Hats of the Pastor's Wife

Pastors' wives, early in their ministry, often feel thrown into a whirlwind of congregational expectations and into the demand of individuals' needs. To find the balance of being "the pastor's wife" and/or "Mommy" in itself yields its own challenges.

If you have already stepped into your ministry of the "pastor's wife" I am sure you will agree that you learn quickly about the *many* hats you have to wear. Or, maybe I should rephrase as, are *expected* to wear, whether they fit or not?

I am sure you must be wondering, *Why do people think that she is to be a jack-of-all-trades*? And *What are the many hats of the pastor's wife*?

Years ago, most people felt that the pastor's wife must play the piano. They assumed piano playing went with the turf, and God forbid if you could not. In fact, it was often one of the questions posed in the pastor's interview.

Often there is a concept that the pastor's wife must also know how to teach Bible studies, oversee Children's Church, Bus Ministry, Street Ministry, Door to Door and Evangelism Outreach, Youth Ministry, Women's Ministry, Single's Ministry, and not to forget, the Married Couples' Events. They believe you should be able to not only plan special events, but market them as well. *Wow! Just to write all of the above was overwhelming! However, do not run off just yet!*

If you *do* play the piano, then someone may delegate you to lead the praise and worship team. *Hey, if the hat fits, where it, right? No, not always.* So often, we "pastors' wives" tend not to take into consideration the fact that we have had no training or experience in certain areas. Instead, we are more apt to grab the hat, throw it on, and attempt to conquer whatever it is that needs to be done.

Sometimes, there is a gifting in an area that God desires to stir the talent He's placed inside of you purposed for His glory. Once accepting the task, we often grow by grace and through the gifting into an incredible woman of God, ushering others into the presence of God.

Know that some hats are just for a season. God requests that anything we do, we do it with thanksgiving unto him at all times, and do all things with excellence (meaning the best you can possibly do). If you find that you do not have the gift or grace for a specific task, do not be ashamed. There are times that God will extend grace to a person to wear a hat until the proper person for the position comes along. Once you decide to move on, keep a watchful eye out for one in your group who *does* have the gift in that particular area. Take the time to mentor them and guide and encourage them until you feel the time has come to release this individual into that area.

There comes a time, especially during the early stages of ministry, when you, as the pastor's wife, are finding your place in the Body of Christ as well. Generally speaking, you have accepted the position, and know the call of God is on your life. Sometimes you will go through trial and error as you seek to find your God given place.

Another hat that the pastor's wife is often forced to wear and accept, is the position of a *counselor.* People usually find it easy to pour their heart out to the pastor's wife, especially if you are a compassionate person. If you are a good listener, it justifies their ease even further. The perfect ingredients are "compassion" for God's people and the "desire to listen." Oftentimes they do not really want answers, but simply enjoy having someone to listen to them. Then the compassion is like icing on the cake. Again, some pastors' wives sincerely have a heart and call for this area, so they find it easy to love and listen.

There are some pastor's wives that do not have the gift of counseling. They may tend to often feel like people are using her to get to her husband, or feel that she is being "dumped on." There needs to be some discernment here and the pastor needs to observe and make the proper shifting to the staff member that does have the true "counseling" gift.

As the pastor's wife, you should only wear the hats that have the proper fit. Wearing a hat too small or too large will leave you feeling frustrated and angry. I can assure you that you will only feel fulfilled when you find the perfect *fit.*

The pastor needs to be sensitive in this area. Allow him to love, lead, and guide you to the proper area of calling that is on your life. By doing so, he will ensure you are set according to the God given gift placed inside of you.

Through prayer, God will give you the completion and fulfillment by leading you to the *hat* that's waiting for you. Rest assured, only *you* can wear your hat as it was tailor-made just for you; wrapped in your genuine calling.

*"Stand therefore, having girded your
waist with truth,
having put on the breastplate of
righteousness,"*
-Ephesians 6:14 (NKJV)

Chapter Three

You've Got To Roll with the Punches

Early in my childhood, at an evening church service, the altar call had been given and I went forward. I rose up from the altar weeping, as I had just been baptized with the Holy Spirit and called into the ministry at the young age of eight. I told my mother and grandmother that God had called me to be either a "Pastor's Wife" or a "Missionary's Wife." I knew beyond the shadow of a doubt I had been called. Today I am walking in both of those callings! Children *can* hear from God!

Born in the country and raised on a farm, I was used to helping with chores, baling hay, driving the tractor in the fields and many other things on my parent's farm. Needless to say, it was quite a culture shock for me moving from the country to my husband's home town. I went from roads that were not even paved, to a major city, which was only a bridge away from Philadelphia, the

City of Brotherly Love. About the only thing I had going for me was I had been raised in a small country church, came from a strong Christian family, and my grandmother was a minister who pastored a church in Lisbon, N.H. She was a strong, Godly influence in my life.

Though our church was a small, country church, I had been active in music, youth, and church activities my entire life. When I married my husband my life took a huge leap into ministry, in things I had never seen, heard of, or experienced! Young and with strong feelings of inadequacy, he tried to gently ease me into my new role as the "pastor's wife."

Back in the 70's we were in an associate pastor position and were over Bus and Youth Ministry. Just married, this was a major adjust-ment in my life. Early in our ministry, one of the many *hats* I had to wear was the *Bus Ministry* hat. I had never heard of such a thing, so this was all new to me. My husband was such a tender teacher and would tell me about bus ministries in larger churches around the United States.

Two ministries parallel to one another were the Bus Ministry and Door to Door invitations.

As I became more experienced, we learned the concept to always go together in teams of two. We were a team. Faithfully, every Saturday morning, we had teams that would operate Door to Door ministry in housing projects and apartments.

One particular day, we decided to make things progress a little faster. Our plan was to cover more ground by knocking on doors directly across the street from one another; this way we could cover two houses at the same time. As I was approaching a house I could hear arguing from inside. I boldly walked up to the door and before I could knock, we were caught off guard by a loud *bang!* A gun had been fired! We both took off running towards each other. It wasn't long before police cars that seemed as if they were flying approached with their lights on and sirens blasting to answer a domestic dispute.

Once things settled down we did not let this detour us; we continued to knock on doors inviting people to church. God blessed the Bus Ministry and many came to the Lord and to the church as a result. This was a seasonal *hat*.

We also had the opportunity to serve as youth ministers. We started out with 12 teens and within a very short time the Lord added and we eventually were ministering to 120 teenagers. Our duties also included picking teenagers up in our church van so that they could come to the youth services.

One of our teens was from a very unsafe area in Camden, N.J. You know, it is not the best place to be late at night when there is a 10pm curfew for the entire city. We had taken the young lady to her home located on top of a Harley Davidson motorcycle shop, at about 11:30pm. My husband got out to walk her to her door, and waited until her parents ushered her in the house. He returned to the church van that we were riding in, and proceeded to make a U turn in a little alley that we frequently turned around in. Out of nowhere we heard gunshots and bullets ricocheting off of the brick walls. With the pedal to the metal and prayers raised to the heavens, we were able to get out safely.

We often laugh about that experience to this day. Praise God that He truly has His Hand on those He calls to do His Kingdom Business.

During that time, I was also introduced to Street Ministry. We would go to shopping centers and parks to hand out tracks and witness to people. Sometimes we would take along a guitar and have our youth service sitting on blankets in parks; with hopes to attract a small crowd. We led people to the Lord and would get their names and addresses so that we could pick them up for church the following Sunday. During this time of ministry, I found this was truly one of my gifts and continue to have a love for Street Ministry to this day. *Outreach and Evangelism* quickly became one of the hats I felt called to wear.

Years later we moved to the Carolina's into a growing and established TV Ministry. At that time, our children were still small, but I accepted the hat of launching as well as teaching a weekly ladies' Bible study at the church we were attending. To my surprise, God blessed it and it grew quickly. We saw many prayers answered.

I also became involved in what we called a *Jesus rock band,* named "The Castaway's Band." We reached out monthly with Prison Ministry in various prisons as well as performed at youth events. Through this ministry, many were saved and it was a very fulfilling experience that I was involved in for many years.

Later we moved to a fairly large church and accepted the position as pastors. With God's blessing, He added to the church and it grew from 190 to close to 1,000 at its peak.

During this time, I became the praise and worship leader for the church. I was somewhat familiar and had slightly developed this gift through serving as a youth pastor forming small praise bands. It was definitely a challenge to wear this hat, as I had never been officially trained in this field. Knowing that I played several instruments, my husband and Church Board felt there was truly a God given gift for music within me.

The church instruments consisted of only a guitar, a piano, and a tambourine; so initiating them into accepting electric and bass guitars, drums, and synthesizers was a stretch for this church; and a difficult challenge for me as the "pastor's wife." However, once they got away from the traditional *piano and organ sound*, the congregation actually enjoyed this new sound.

God blessed and I led praise and worship in that church for ten plus years.

As a pastor's wife, you must learn to roll with the punches; because it is inevitable they *will* come.

God also uses me to operate in the gift of the *Word of Knowledge*. One morning during praise and worship, I received a Word from the Lord that there were three people in the audience who were struggling with suicidal thoughts. I encouraged them to come forward and we would pray with them and minister to them.

While only two people came forward, my heart was broken for the third. Feeling that it was difficult for them, I felt strong in my spirit that I knew who it was. So with compassion in my heart I said, "I believe I know who you are. I don't want you to leave with these thoughts in your mind, and maybe you don't want to walk up here alone. I will come to you and walk to the altar with you." I walked down to a young lady whom I had never seen before. When I approached her, she agreed it was her and began to weep. She willingly, with relief, walked to the altar. We were able to minister to her and see the Lord touch her life that day.

After praise and worship was over, I slipped out through the choir room door to go to the restroom. As I walked down the hallway, I was approached by a male member of our church. He literally snatched me up, as if by my lapels, and body slammed me against the wall. Dashing over to my aid, our youth pastor instructed him to take his hands off me. Trying to keep his voice to a minimal, and from allowing others to see this episode, our youth pastor asked him to step into an office so we could discuss the situation. He refused.

Amid my husband ministering the Word in the sanctuary, the youth pastor was in the hall trying to protect me, the *pastor's wife,* from this irate church member.

Come to find out, he was a prominent business man in our church and was highly embarrassed and humiliated by the Word of Knowledge that had been spoken. Unbeknownst to me, the young lady I had compassionately walked down to the altar was his daughter, who was visiting from Germany. Though she was fine with the manner in which things were handled, *Daddy was not*.

He demanded an apology be made to the whole congregation. As you can imagine, I was greatly shaken, but attempted to understand his view. I advised him that I would be more than willing to do that; however, he was requesting that I do it *immediately*. After much discussion, the youth pastor and I were able to convince him that we did not need to interrupt the service while the Word was being ministered.

Communion was being served this particular morning. As my husband prepared to present the elements, I went over to the table and softly asked him if I could share something with the church. He looked very puzzled with the approach and timing; however I made it clear through eye contact that *I REALLY NEEDED TO DO THIS NOW!* Graciously he obliged. The offended individual and his family, stood in the very center at the back of the church watching our every move. As they gazed with beady eyes, the father's arms folded across his chest, they listened attentively, waiting to hear what I was going to say.

While interrupting the flow of the service, I gently reminded the audience that I had received a Word of Knowledge during praise and worship that morning. I informed them that unintentionally I had highly offended a family within the church and that I had no intention, whatsoever, of hurting them or that family. I apologized stating how extremely sorry I was; but that I had only wanted the individual to receive the ministry that was being presented. I had no idea she was related to this family. With that said, the whole family proceeded to stamp angrily through the back door of the sanctuary. As if that was not enough, as young pastors, not knowing how to handle the situation, tension continued to mount with this couple.

My husband would console me and remind me to pray for them, that God would deal with them *in time*. This went on for weeks. Knowing now what we learned from this situation, we would have immediately dismissed them.

I learned that as I worked God's process in my own quiet time, indeed, the Lord began to deal with this family. He allowed things to come into their lives to correct them. First, their business caught on fire. Second, his wife received news of cancer.

One Wednesday night at the church I was walking in the hall and this same individual approached me again. Now let me admit, I was a bit apprehensive. He asked me if I could step out of the hallway into the audio room. Cautiously I accepted his request. He explained to me that he was very sorry for the way he had handled the situation with his daughter and wanted to know if I would forgive him. *He had recognized God's dealing.*

God had once again answered our prayers! Not *only* did God restore the relationship between both families, but *Jehovah Rapha (the Lord that Healeth)* had healed his wife of cancer. From that day forward, we have a cordial relationship.

Indeed "Pastor's Wife," *You've Got To Roll With The Punches*. You see, as you *Roll,* you will grow in your walk with the Lord and be an encouragement to others. For the ones that throw *The Punches*, your walk, and *how* you *Roll,* will teach, and speak volumes to them.

"A merry heart does good, like medicine,
But a broken spirit dries the bones."
-Proverbs 17:22 (NKJV)

Chapter Four

LIGHTEN UP

Remember how Aaron and Hur both came up under the arms of Moses? When they held up his hands, Israel prevailed, but if they would have let his hands down, Israel would have lost the battle. (See Exod. 17:8-13.) If you are under a senior leader or pastor, it is essential that *you* keep their hands lifted.

When a team has been called and set to walk with a pastor, it is imperative for them to unite while seeking to accomplish the ONE purpose—*to build the Kingdom of God,* not to be divisive. Walking in unity will require the team to have strong, healthy, functional relationships... *together.*

So that there is ONE focus, each team player must recognize the senior pastor's vision once they hop on board—*to accomplish the heart of the Father.* Oftentimes, people are more interested in *their* "position" rather than the *leader's* "vision." It is extremely difficult when there is a teammate pulling in the opposite direction or trying to achieve *their* vision. God will promote you, in proper time for your season, if you are faithful to the task at hand.

If your vision is not aligned with the covering you are under, you need to seek the Face of God and He will direct you to either move on, or bring yourself under submission to get in line with their vision. God may only have you with this covering, or man/woman of God, for a season. However, God is watching your progress and how well you handle working under authority.

Like a box of chocolates, ministry offers an assortment of challenges; ranging from the congregation to the church staff.

I remember an instance where the need to add to our present staff had become abso-lutely necessary; as God had expanded our congregation rather large. In itself, the church had recognized the need for a unique individual to direct the Music Ministry in its entirety. Not that they were seeking change in the praise and worship area; rather, someone with the ability to oversee: special music, choir, youth music, children's music, musicals, the drama department, and special events as a whole.

For years, as praise and worship leader, I had established and trained the praise and worship team, along with the band as well. Being the praise and worship leader involved preparing for 3 services during the week with rehearsals, along with all the other bells and whistles that came with that role.

In addition, I held the title of *Weekly Women's Bible Study and Intercession Leader,* in conjunction I would also counsel from Monday through Friday. I also oversaw *Evangelism and Outreach,* which required coordinating and leading the actual outreach events. Running on "auto pilot", I was beginning to feel *extreme overload* wearing my many hats simultaneously, including the most important ones, "Wife" and "Mommy."

Might I add, *ALL OF THIS* with *NO PAY* in the early years when the church could not afford to pay me. Whenever this subject was mentioned in leadership meetings, we were informed that the church hired us as "a package."

Yet, until the doors opened to hire; I was determined to *make it work*, regardless! Sometimes you have to stand-in in a particular area until the individual called to that ministry is in place. I poured everything out daily, but God continued to re-fill me.

As I look back, I see how God truly kept me in my "auto-pilot" moments. *Stay with me here… I promise you, the load "lightens up" very soon!*

For twelve years I served and worked diligently with no pay. *I sowed where I wanted to go.* After the twelfth year the church board decided to bring me on as paid staff. We had eventually arrived at the place where our church could financially support the much needed *new* staff. We hired and placed in position the individuals whom we felt would follow the vision; help carry the load, and work together as team players. We were doing great! The Lord had blessed us with a youth minister and children's pastor, just to name a couple of our blessings!

In addition, once a month, we had all-night prayer meetings. I cherished the intimate time spent with God, but there came a point where I could no longer *carry* the load. Emotionally, physically, and mentally it had become extremely draining while trying to accomplish all that was expected of me. By this time, burnout was imminent. I didn't realize my overload breaker was on *tilt.*

Finally, it hit me… *all the fuses in my breaker box had shorted out* and I had come to my breaking point. The rumor mill started flying and I ended up buckling under the weight.

My heart was broken, as the new staff members had no idea what type of person I was. All they were seeing was this *burn-out pastor's wife* side. That was not me at all.

At this time, the season for our current youth minister was also coming to a close. He had only been with us for six months and indeed was an incredible singer. A known singing tour group called him and offered him a position. This young man was indeed gifted and it was quite evident that God had other plans for him. He accepted their offer, therefore moving on to his next season.

So the transition was a bit of a boat-rocker for our congregation, as they had grown to love him and his family, and appreciated his gift and talent.

Once again, the old rumor mill started churning again. This is a difficult thing for leadership to tolerate when your church may already be on shaky ground, due to so many changes.

Much to our delight, our children's pastor administrator stayed. *Together,* with God on our side, we withstood some difficult challenges and changes. However, once things appeared to settle down, and the staff was in its rightful position, things flowed smoothly for a while.

I highly recommend reading the book, *Honor's Reward* by John Bevere. This is an excellent resource for anyone in ministry today. Once my husband and I read it, we discovered what a tool it was and how it could have really mentored and prepared us early in our ministry.

To reiterate what was stated earlier in the chapter I want to ask this question:

"Are you following the 'vision' of the Leadership or have you gained a 'position' under him that you do not want to lose? Again... are you following the vision, or the position?"

Consider your answer and let's look at a perfect Biblical example; as I am in agreement with John Bevere's concept on this as well.

In the book of Numbers in the Bible, we read where Moses and the children of Israel wandered in the desert for forty years. During that time, Moses did not have a Jewish wife; instead he took an Ethiopian woman to marry. However, Miriam, appearing to be quite the opinionated woman, strongly objected to his decision. Therefore, she and Aaron spoke against Moses with an opinion and complaint. (See Num. 12.)

If you study this passage you will find that the root of this problem was their jealousy of Moses' influence on the people and his position. You can see this clearly in verse 2.

"So they said, Has the LORD indeed spoken only through Moses? Has he not spoken through us also? And the LORD heard it".

-Numbers 12:2 (NKJV)

Again, "And the Lord heard it."

They could find no fault with Moses' leadership so they chose to come against his wife. Sound familiar? This is an age old problem, ladies. Miriam was obviously struggling with pride and jealousy. You can see that God strongly opposes and hates this type of attitude. He deals with it directly Himself.

As a pastor's wife reading the *Miriam* context, in comparison to our own issues, we so often take the heat for things that we have no involvement with. *That is a whole different subject matter in itself. I could write a book on that statement alone.*

I will leave the rest for you to read and study, but please *heed* this lesson from Numbers 12. The Word of God does not change. God strictly deals with individuals who try to take a position He did not give them. He also deals with those who come against the leader or Leadership whom He, Himself has appointed.

In the book of Ecclesiastes 1:9, the Word says "there is no new thing under the sun." As I stated before, if you no longer can support the vision, then it is time for you to transition.

It had always been my desire to develop healthy and lasting relationships with our staff. With all that had occurred with the transition in our church, it had been very stressful on our church leadership and Leadership. We wore stress and tension like a coat, and countenances were revealing much heaviness. One day I decided we needed to *lighten up*.

So I armed myself from the local store with water pistols and large water guns. Feeling like the Lone Ranger, I filled them with water and trotted down to their offices. I declared, "Ok guys, we need to lighten up around here!" At that moment I began to shoot them with water pistols. They started to laugh and then charged out the door chasing after me. One grabbed the water hose while another held me and I was hosed down! It was hilarious! Needless to say, it definitely accomplished the purpose of *lightening things up* and they still laugh about it to this day.

So many times we are under stress in a working relationship. We need to not only take time to laugh but we need to *make* people laugh. The Word is true, "A merry heart does good, like a medicine…" (Prov. 17:22 NKJV).

Even if you have to break out with the "Lone Ranger" act and you and Tonto put together a plan; it is well worth it as you will literally see the tension lift.

The Lord had unzipped the *old stress and tension coat* our leadership had been wearing; and replaced it with a *peaceful, energized sweat suit.* We were ready to get back in the gym and new precedence had been set: *lighten up, roll with the punches, and get your focus back!*

"… so the service of the house of the LORD was set in order."
-II Chronicles 29:35 (NKJV)

Chapter Five

The Pastor's Home

My husband and I desired to create a healthy atmosphere for our marriage and children. Early in our ministry, we established an agreement that our home would be our family's place of solace and refuge. It was our *home*; the place where we loved, laughed, cried, and sighed, without being in the fishbowl of ministry. We could kick off our shoes, put on our t-shirts and shorts, and enjoy the relationships within our own home.

In our first inner-city church we were blessed to live in the church parsonage, which was connected to the church. Though it came with benefits, it also had its drawbacks as well. Since "the pastor's home" is usually under great scrutiny and the watchful eye, we chose to purchase our own home away from the church grounds. Not only did this create balance, but also helped to establish proper boundaries for the congregation.

Similar to a doctor's schedule, pastors are usually on call twenty-four hours a day. Not to sound discourteous, but we were thrilled when answering machines were introduced. With the large amount of telephone calls we received, we were then able to screen them. We quickly learned that many of the calls should be re-routed to the church. This took a little training at first, but we were gentle with the callers and redirected them to the church secretary.

We desired privacy as much as possible; as you may already be aware, a pastor's life is pretty full. Once we obtained that privacy, we worked diligently to protect it.

It is essential that you create proper balance and boundaries *in* your home and *for* your home, as this is a very important factor for everyone. Your family along with your church family will appreciate the consistency in this area, as it is fairly easy to maintain the majority of the time. However, there are always the occasional emergencies that you will experience as the "pastors". Over time, this *balance* will prove to be a blessing.

It appeared the preceding pastor did not institute business hours within the church. However, this is important to establish for a growing church. The Church needs to feel assured that the pastor can be reached and is accessible during a set schedule noted as "regular business hours."

If you are, in addition to your position at the church, also engaged in employment outside of the church, then proper protocol would be to make known your availability, your location and contact information.

The outcome here is *trust*. Not only can you now be easily reached, but you have created balance for you and your family, and time to connect with the sheep as their shepherd desires. Remember to be consistent, so they will know where, when and how to reach you.

The pastor's home needs to be a place for him/her to feel content, to relax and rest, or prop their feet up and watch a football game if they so desire. His/her private time needs to be protected, honored, and respected. Generally speaking, if he is meeting the needs and demands of the congregation, day in and day out, then it should be understood and honored that his home is his place of retreat, *without disturbances*, except in the case of an emergency.

You and the pastor need to create the boundary and raise the standard to protect one another's time and space. Unfortunately, there are always a handful of people that will try to use you, as the "pastor's wife," only to get to the pastor. Do not take offense to this, as this type of situation arises in every church. However, if you and the pastor will stand together, you will recognize this *handful's approach* early on; so this generally will not become a problem.

"What about the pastor's home and visitors?" you might ask. You *can* and *need to* have friends over. Sometimes it's good to remember that *we have a life too*. There is nothing wrong with fellowship or entertaining your friends, as most pastors and their wives desire to have this time. However, be wise and selective about the people you invite to hang out at your "haven".

A good rule of thumb is to NOT advertise to the Church who is coming over to your house for a cook-out or other type of fellowship, as this could create unnecessary rifts and tension for those who may not be invited. Please use wisdom and balance in this area.

Any functions that involve large groups should always be held at the church, church grounds, or choice destination for events. Keep your selected list of personal friends small. I promise you, you *won't* regret it!

"Her children rise up and call her blessed;
Her husband also, and he praises her"
-Proverbs 31:28 (NKJV)

Chapter Six

Family Matters

Once we got things in order with our house, it became not only our "home", but a "haven." We tried to keep a schedule for our family and found that this was a good regiment for our sons as they were growing up. It helped to create a sense of love and stability.

In the elementary years, breakfast was a daily routine of ours as well. Not Pop Tart's while heading out the door, but we enjoyed a sit-down breakfast with the whole family. Each morning afterwards, we would spend time with God together. We read from a children's devotional and prayed with them before they went to school. In due course they had learned the importance of prayer.

One morning we woke up late and were rushing to get to school. We had an accident on the way there and the children were quick to announce, "Mom, we didn't have our prayer time this morning to ask God to cover us with the Blood today!" *My, my, my… "out of the mouth of babes".* I realized the accident could have been worse and I praise God that He did have his hand on us. However, it was definitely a learning experience from both sides of the coin.

We were very consistent in teaching our children the importance of having a personal relationship with God. We aimed to encourage and enlighten them by teaching them in a fun and pleasant atmosphere. We never let our time with God become a habit, instead, each day brought on a fresh approach.

Not only does the pastor's home need to be a place of refuge for the pastor and his wife, but for the sake of the children as well. They need to have time with just Dad and Mom, and they need to know they are high on the list with their parents.

A guideline that we established early in our home was the *Proper Priority for Pastors and Leadership in Ministry,* based upon Scripture.

For the pastor and the pastor's wife it is as follows:

God's Divine Order:

(1) Your relationship with God
(2) Your relationship with your mate
(3) Your relationship with your children
(4) Ministry, and so forth

We have practiced this *priority list* throughout our marriage and found that if any one of these guidelines moves out of order, it ALWAYS causes a problem. Once we set things back in proper alignment everything else falls right into place. These priorities always work because it is God's Divine Order. When we step out of the Divine Order it is felt all the way down the line.

We have one particular memory that our family still laughs about, even unto this day. "Mommy" was hurrying to serve breakfast and everyone had their juice but "Daddy." I quickly grabbed what I had *thought* was Apple Juice out of the refrigerator and poured it in his glass. He took a drink and all of a sudden he started spraying his mouthful of "drink," gasping, and gagging. The boys were laughing hysterically. To all of our amazement, I had mistakenly grabbed the Apple Cider Vinegar. Our whole family roared with laughter all the way to school that day. We told him, "Now you know how Jesus felt!" What a great memory of laughter in our home around the breakfast table.

Another area of concern with your family is *support*. There may be a member in your church who truly desires to serve you as the pastor's wife. They may be one who serves in many capacities; one to include, ringing your doorbell... early in the morning... offering to clean your house, cook a meal, babysit, or do the laundry. As this could seem to be an inconvenience, this truly is a blessing and can accommodate in lightening your load as a pastor's wife, as well as ensuring your children are taken care of and the house stays in order. This support can allow you to take care of your *to do* list or handle anything that needs attention at church.

Some people have the gift of caring for your children. They are called to do this and sincerely love it.

(Be sure to check out anyone who is offering to care for your children, due to the day and age

in which we live. Background checks are easy to do and affordable. They definitely are worth the investment.)

Then you have those who want to get close to the "pastor's family" no matter what it takes. They will try every conceivable tactic known. They may or may not be the right person God has chosen to serve along side, so be very discerning. To serve the pastor and his family, it is a high calling and this person needs to be extremely loyal and supportive.

On another note, anyone involved in the ministry knows that your house can quickly become Grand Central Station if you let it. It is normal for "the preacher's kid(s)" to want to interact with other children in the church. They may be invited over to someone's house for the afternoon or a sleepover.

We allowed this privilege, as it is normal and healthy for children to interact with their own age group of peers. We once had a season where they were requesting to have friends over just about every Sunday. So we established a rule with them: "I will always try to say 'yes' to your request as much as possible, but if I say 'no,' do not stand there and beg in front of your friend. If I say 'no' there is a reason. But I will always try to say 'yes' so that you can have fun on Sunday afternoons, too." We only had one incident of "begging" to occur, but we stood by our rules.

I was one who wanted to know where my children were and what they were doing at all times; so we would check on them periodically, regardless if they were in their room playing or at a friend's house. This "Sunday playtime" worked very well for our family; they were happy and we were happy. It kept them busy on Sunday afternoons and we were able to have time for us as well.

Our children grew up appreciating the ministry, as they were loved and respected from others. We taught them to always be grateful; and because they were the "pastor's sons," indeed, they were definitely special, but to always value the privilege. We trained them while they were young, that special things, presents, and gifts were just that... *special*. We informed our sons to never just "expect" things because of who they are, that people were not obligated to give unto them, but did so because they wanted to bless them. They learned to always be appreciative and thankful regardless. "Always have the attitude of gratitude."

The weekends were always our time set aside for one another. Every Friday night was "family night." We always did special things with our kids. We would usually stay in and pop popcorn, drink soda and watch something exciting on TV, or play games. Then Saturday would be our "family day." Seldom did we deviate from this as we had set aside this day for *our* day together. We took mountain trips, Discovery Place trips, Zoo Trips, hikes, water sports, and much more. We let our boys know that they were number one to us even above ministry. There were times, occasionally, when we would attend a wedding or a funeral, etc. however any time we lost with them, we were always sure to redeem. This was very important to us.

We listened to them with an open heart and tried to love and guide them into whatever God called them to be. Whether it was a plumber, electrician or super-man, it did not matter; as long as they knew they were walking in what God called them to be. It was understood, so we never had to force them to go to church. We never forced them to be involved; we just loved, guided, trained, and lead them.

We also included our children in ministry opportunities at very young ages. Our oldest started drum lessons at the age of three and was playing drums full time for our praise and worship services at seven years old. What a gift! Both of our sons became involved in the Children's Ministry as soon as they were old enough to handle responsibility. This taught them how to learn and grow under leaders, as well as the ministry aspect of it. They grew up loving church and ministry.

Today, my little drummer boy and his younger brother are still walking in ministry. They individually accepted the call of God on their lives to minister in leading Praise and Worship, and working in other capacities on the pastoral staff of two great and unique and dynamic churches.

Children need to feel that they are not just on the side line of the family or ministry, but rather a key player on the team. Make certain they feel loved and nurtured, as you give guidance and release responsibility at the appropriate time. This encourages them and teaches them the Heart of the Father in a positive way.

"He heals the brokenhearted And binds up their wounds."

-Psalm 147:3 (NKJV)

Chapter Seven

Sheep Bites and Bandages

I Peter 4:12-14 says:

> *"Beloved, do not think it strange concerning the fiery trial which is to try you, as though some strange thing happened to you; but rejoice to the extent that you partake of Christ's sufferings, that when His glory is revealed, you may also be glad with exceeding joy. If you are reproached for the name of Christ, blessed are you, for the Spirit of glory and of God rests upon you. On their part He is blasphemed, but on your part He is glorified"* (NKJV).

*C*hurch people can be the most precious people on the face of the earth. Some never cause a bit of trouble, while at times it appears that others have the "thorn-in-the-flesh" ministry.

In the ministry, you have to learn how to shrug things off, or as stated in Chapter 3, "roll with the punches." Since we are all human, this can be difficult at times, because *God* has created us to be emotional beings. If you are a person of compassion, there are times when you find yourself misunderstood. The misunder-standings, can lead to wounds, or as I like to call them, *sheep bites.*

There is nothing worse than a sheep bite. Sometimes it may barely knick the skin and then there are times a bite can seep to the bone. You try to forgive, you try to love, all the while this sheep bite becomes nasty and very painful. Initially one stings; and as the days go by, if it is not truly given to God, it will become infected. If it is not properly dealt with according to the Word, it will heal, but it will heal with a scar. The sad part is, if it is not healed properly, when bumped or scraped with a similar situation, generally, there will be a recurrence.

Sometimes, in smaller churches particu-larly, staff people have their own hidden, secret agenda.

Years ago, while co-pastoring with my husband, there was a season where I felt like a moving target. We had experienced issues with some of our staff, and rather than coming along side *with* us, they formed sides *against* us. It was very hurtful, very damaging, and discordant. It became quite evident that they certainly did, indeed, have their own agenda, and eventually God exposed it.

On this occasion, one associate pastor became good friends with another pastor. *Now I will be the first to tell you that there is nothing wrong with that in itself; in fact, we highly encourage relationships within the staff.* As their friendship grew, they began to share more and more amongst themselves. Then the domino effect kicked in.

It wasn't long before invisible walls were formed and distance was created between them and the senior pastor and his wife. *Do you see the adversary had a plan here?* Then they began to attract friends in the church that were on "their" side. *Since when do we have sides? Were we not suppose to be a team who was joined together to work for ONE purpose, the SAME purpose? What was happening?*

Personal plans and secret agendas began to brew. Soon they came to the pastor and Board with, "Pastor, we feel God is telling us to start a church in this city on the other side of town." This can happen and it could be a good thing, but the spirit behind this was not formed with the right heart. There was an underlying spirit called *selfish ambition*.

After many meetings, the pastor determined that in order to protect the mother church, we needed to release them and with blessing. Leadership knew if they kept their heart and attitude right, God would bless our church.

They left and took one hundred people with them. It was a rough transition for our church. When these things happen you have to ride them out. God's grace will sustain you.

It was very hurtful as the pastor's wife, because I had good relationships with some of the people, prior to the scattering of sheep. This was one of those incidents where we *chose to love regardless*. God indeed blessed us and continued to meet every need.

As this pastor left and started the "church plant", it was not long until the very sheep that loved and supported him began to buck and bite him. Sad to say, the church lasted a few years, and the pastor, unto this day, has not returned to pastoring.

Sheep bites and bandages. It is essential for the pastor's wife to have her own relationship with God. Every day spend time with God. Every day! Read the Word and develop your prayer walk personally. If you fail to do this, you may survive the small bites but you will not subdue the bites that sink to the bone.

You may have the right intentions to clear up a situation or to be the peacemaker, only to find that sometimes, the other party has no intentions of honoring your attempt of reconciliation. God knows your heart and He will honor your attempt rather they receive or reject it. You may walk away with another bite and go home and shed a few more tears. But you must know in your heart that you have done the right thing, and that the Lord is pleased with your effort.

You will have people that will love you one minute and strongly dislike you the next. In the call of the pastor's wife, we often feel like we are "bit" with the *revolving target syndrome*. There are times we get bit with issues and obstacles, therefore, taking the blame for things we are not even aware of.

One year my husband and I decided to take a trip to the mountains to spend three days fasting and praying for our personal direction and that of our church. While there, I was struggling with some of those sheep bites. I had so many emotional bandages I felt like I was bleeding to death. While in prayer I heard the Lord specifically say, "KARYL, I HAVE CALLED YOU HERE TO *LEAD* THEM, NOT TO BE THEIR FRIEND." That statement set me free! He also said, "*I* WILL GIVE YOU FRIENDS." I took my Rhema Word from the Lord seriously, and from that day forward, I made the distinction between MY heart and the LORD'S ministry. Because He cared enough to make an enormous impact on my perspective of ministry, for this I will forever be grateful.

When we returned home from God healing my emotional wounds, lo and behold, we received word that a mass exodus had begun.

About twenty-five people were leaving to move on to another church. In that group of people, was my best friend and her husband.

The test came immediately after I had received the specific Word from the Lord. Even though, we received yet another puncture wound returning from a fast, we did not lose sight of what God had given us. We felt that God was pruning back to bear more fruit.

Indeed, the very next Sunday we began to have a move of God unlike anything we had ever seen. It began with a prayer meeting, then Bible study with both men and women attending. For a long time we did not announce the meetings. The people would approach us after every service and ask, "Can we do this again tomorrow night?"

This sovereign move of God lasted two and a half years. It was incredible! People were saved, healed and delivered. Services went unending day in and day out. There came a point when we had to literally schedule days off, for the people and for our family.

We eventually migrated to an "Hour of Power," once a week during lunch hour in place of the evening services every night.

The *mass exodus* that had left clearly resulted in Revival and fresh fruit produced. I recently received an email from someone who had been saved and dramatically changed during that move of God; and they are still loving and serving God unto this day.

That "best friend" is still my best friend today, but God was leading her and her husband in a new direction. We accepted and received their decision without hurt feelings. They came and talked with us and shared their heart. We discerned that God desired to do "a new thing" in their lives, therefore, we were able to release them with blessing.

God will always take the *bad* and work it for your *good*, resulting in the *good times* far outweighing the *bad*. God is faithful at healing and binding up the brokenhearted.

Sometimes the "brokenhearted" is the shepherd or the "wife" of the shepherd. Don't allow the bandages to suffocate the bites and prevent healing. As I stated earlier, they will fester again when simply bumped or scraped if we don't deal with them properly. If we don't expose and disinfect a cut, hurt can easily set in and turn into bitterness.

"Looking carefully lest anyone fall short of the grace of God; lest any root of bitterness springing up cause trouble, and by this many become defiles;" (Heb.12:15, N KJV).

God does not want His leaders walking around with sheep bites and bandages. Go to your Healer. Let God minister to you and heal your wounds. In return, when you minister, you will release healing on a new level, like never before.

"That the genuineness of your faith, being much more precious than gold that perishes, though it is tested by fire, may be found to praise, honor, and glory at the revelation of Jesus Christ, whom having not seen you love. Though now you do not see Him, yet believing, you rejoice with joy inexpressible and full of glory,"
-I Peter 1:7-8 (NKJV)

*"And let us not grow weary while doing good, for in due season
we shall reap if we do not lose heart."*
-Galatians 6:9 (NKJV)

Chapter Eight

Spiritual Leeches

In previous chapters, you've read where I referred to the *counseling hat* we wear as the pastor's wife. However, I am not exactly sure why *we* are the chosen few who are saddled with too much counseling. Perhaps with our caring hearts God equipped us with, it just fits *us* a little better.

Counseling seems to come with the "Pastor and Pastor's Wife" package. Overall, it really is not a difficult task, as basically you are lending an ear to people's problems and guiding them to focus on God and His Word for their answers. I have seen many people grow spiritually as a direct result of encouraging them and giving them the right tools to develop their own walk with the Lord.

Every now and then you will come across, what I call, a "spiritual leech." I don't know why it is, but every church seems to have its share.

This type of person is one who comes crying on your shoulder every time they see you, and are not willing to follow through with the process and direction that you have given them.

In our ministry many years ago, I counseled three people at one time with this "leech-a-lot" condition. *Talking about ready to throw the hat in?* All three were single women and had their own unique problems. One had been deeply involved in a cult, witchcraft and Satanism. She was a teenage, "pastor's kid" that had become very rebellious and was causing her family much heartache. Her parents were at their wits end and were desperate for her to be helped. I took her on as my project because I have a passion for working with street people and *the down and outers*.

Needless to say, this girl's life clearly was a mess. I desired to work with her and help pull her out of the *pit* she had gotten herself into.

One night I stayed up all night ministering and praying with her. God then set her free! It was so beautiful to see the change in her countenance and watch her sprout and begin to grow. Unfortunately, it lasted about four months, when she called me and told me, "I just can't hang with this kind of living."

I told her very firmly that God had delivered her from some very strong demonic holds in her life. I explained to her that if she chose to walk away, she would suffer very serious consequences for her decision.

This was the only instance where I had ever felt like God was going to deliver her over to a reprobate mind if she went the direction she was choosing.

It was heartbreaking to see her walk away, move back in with a fifty year old pimp, and watch her young life spiral downward once again.

A few months later, we received word that she was back on drugs and running the streets, while turning tricks for this pimp. My heart went out for her, but I realized, unless a person wants **change** for **themself**, there is nothing you, me, nor anyone can do to help bring about this change. *They* have to want God for themselves!

I was teaching a ladies' Bible study and was in the middle of sharing the Word, when this same girl literally came busting in the door, whaling a knife and coming at me. I was not scared at all but started to move towards her telling the women to pray. I was pleading the Blood of Jesus as I moved easily in her direction.

She began to shake and cry, and her hands shook as she continued to thrust the knife toward me. I just kept pleading the Blood of Jesus over and over, and suddenly she began to shake uncontrollably, she dropped the knife and ran out the back door. Little did she know that the police had been called and were waiting outside of the very door she ran out.

Needless to say, the little old ladies that were present in the prayer group were a bit shook up, but I loved on them and talked to them and reassured them that everything was okay; and that we needed to pray that this young lady's eyes would be opened.

There came a point when I realized she no longer wanted help, but was merely thriving on the attention. At this point, I had to divert my attention to those who were not spiritual leeches, but who truly desired to change; and do whatever it took to see it manifest.

Unto this day, it hurts me to say that she has never returned to God. Although, now in her thirties, she looks as if she is sixty years old. Her countenance now displays the weathered looked of sin.

Most people are generally willing to work with the Leadership and do what is required to see their lives change and move in a new direction. These are the ones you enjoy pouring yourself into because they allow God to change and rearrange their lives. They become God's trophies and He receives all the glory.

At the same time, we had two other single young ladies in our church that were also demanding much attention. I was young and still learning, however, I poured myself into counseling sessions with these two individually, and saw changes that encouraged me enough to keep meeting with them on a weekly basis. But eventually, it reached the point that I simply dreaded seeing them even come toward me at any church function. They had become extremely needy and demanding of my time.

After a season of really working with them for several years, along with some other caring ladies in our church that had counseled them, we sought the Lord as what our next steps should be. *I loved His answer.*

After talking with each one and them, seeing the need in their lives, they understood and agreed that they needed to move to the next level. Our Church helped make arrangements and I personally took them on a shopping spree and purchased additional clothes for them. I put them on a bus and sent them to Teen Challenge for a year.

Interested to see the continued process of both ladies? One completed the program and went to work with Teen Challenge. Then God elevated her to a position with the Joyce Meyer Ministries for several years. It has been such a blessing to see the Lord work in her life as she made choices that caused her to progress forward in her walk with the Lord and in the ministry as well.

The other young lady stayed in the program, but unfortunately went backwards instead of forwards. She never grasped what the Lord was trying to do in her life and remains in the same rut today.

"Spiritual leeches" can really cause a huge weight to sit on the pastor's wife. There is a fine line of caring so much about people that you can't bear the thought of letting go because of what their future could hold. God did not call you to be their babysitter; He called you to be their leader. Sometimes you can gently nudge and then other times you must thrust people in the right direction; but at the end of the day you MUST leave the results to the Lord.

Something that turned out to be a lifesaver for me was something I requested people to do when I counseled with them. I would have them pick up a spiral bound notebook and I assigned them homework. If they came back on their next visit and did not have their homework completed in their notebook, I would give them another chance to catch up and bring it in the following week. If they came again without their notebook, then I knew that they were not serious and were just spiritual leeches trying to take from my time and energy that needed to be poured elsewhere.

Pastors' wives need to be very discerning with those that God has entrusted in your care.

Work with people who really want to change and move forward in their destiny, but for those who are just spiritual leeches…keep on moving! God called you to lead them not drag them.

*"An excellent wife is the crown of her husband,
But she who causes shame is like
rottenness in his bones."*

-Proverbs 12:4 (NKJV)

Chapter Nine

Hello… I Have My Own Identity

As a pastor's wife, you may find yourself struggling with the feeling that you've lost your *own* personal identity. People most often address and identify you as, "Oh, you're the pastor's wife?" In the early years of marriage this usually does not bother us; in fact, we're rather fond of being identified with our husband as "his wife." Several years pass and after numerous sheep bites, after wearing many hats, once we've mastered how to roll with the punches, and have learned to lighten up, there generally comes a time when the "pastor's wife" would like to develop *her own identity*.

In the past you've taken on the role of Wife, Mom, and *Whatever Your Gifts Are*. But now you have come to the realization that God made YOU who YOU are. So then the question comes, "God, who am I?" "Why am I here?" "Where am I going?"

Being a pastor's wife we often accept our title and role graciously. We are thankful that God has chosen us to walk along side our mate and play the supportive role. We are grateful for the opportunity the Lord has given us as we've felt the union of two lives become one.

Many women want their own personal identity and *it is possible* to have it back again, I promise you. We desire to be accepted and recognized for who we are and what we accomplish through the grace of God. It is clear that you can lose your own identity while being one with your mate, but it's okay. God has instilled in us the "know how" to have our own identity as well as carry the identity of our husband, both at the same time.

He truly amazes me!

Your husband can assist and be very inspirational in the role of clarifying your identity as YOU.

Now let's take it a little deeper. The Bible says that we are made in the image of God. Praise is a part of God's nature and He desires to be praised. Since we are made in His image, then praise will encourage and motivate *us* to the next level in Him. We do not work to be praised, but thankfulness and encouragement stoke the fire of progress and somehow projects us forward for the next new project.

Each person has been equipped with a gift and in some cases more than one. God made it this way to compliment one another. You should evaluate and check your heart to ensure that the motive behind developing your own identity is purely to understand who you are in God and not to cause division between you and your husband. God has created you both to be a team. He has no desire for either of you to be competitive, but complimentary of one another. Your goal and purpose should be to expand the Kingdom of God **together**.

Working as a team will result in your ministry being far more effective. You can and should raise up others who have the same or similar gifts to build a strong team in the Army of the Lord.

God formed you and created you long ago and I cannot stress enough that your life's purpose is about the Kingdom of God. He created you with your gifts solely to mirror His Kingdom. We should never forget that we are Ambassadors for Christ and the message should remain pure and simple. We should have no agenda, but His.

When you were born again, you became one in Christ. As you develop your own identity, it will be separate from your mate's as you are two individuals, but the two shall become one. You are connected to your husband and his name and his ministry. This does not in any way weaken your own identity but strengthens it.

Most of you have heard of ministries wherein the husband and wife started and grew it *together*. Over time, speaking engagements and demands on each individual's separate lives and identity transpired. Everything seemed to flow for a while, but then the demanding sched-ules and travel became a divisive tool for the enemy; causing a very strong and solid ministry to slowly deteriorate at the seams. The enemy moved in with great intensity and over a period of time eroded the fiber of their marriage, team, and ministry; dissolving these relationships down to nothing.

Once they recognized this *set-up,* in some cases, each party would try to hang on with every ounce of strength they had to their *own ministry.* They would try to savor the remains of a sinking ship, yet still blinded as to what had initially taken place. Granted, some have salvaged there identity but their ministries each have taken serious hits and are not impacting the Kingdom to the degree they once did **together** as a team, the way *God* intended!

It can be very tedious and a strategic challenge to maintain proper balance in your relationship. However, God will always sustain you if you allow Him. You must maintain balance as ONE so that you both can continue to minister in strength and full power to effectively impact the Kingdom.

Reproach to the King's name does damage. Do everything within your personal power to maintain balance in your walk with God, your marriage, your family, and *then* your ministry; in that proper biblical order. If you allow any of these to get out of line and order, there will be consequences that could have been avoided. Always remember "therefore what God has joined together, let not man separate" (Matt. 19:6, NKJV).

Seek to bring honor to the Name of Jesus and not reproach. Your *own identity* is not worth sacrificing the *whole* for a *part*. Operate in integrity and work together as mates to maintain healthy relationships between the two of you.

Nothing displeases God more than to bring two people together, pour blessings on their ministry, honor them and give them individual ministries; and in return, they let down their guard and allow the enemy to sneak in, as the world sits back and mocks the model of marriage in the church world. It takes work from both parties, but it is not impossible.

It is so important to remember **balance**. Schedule time together in your appointment books and do not allow anything to cancel it. Do not compete against each other. Without one another, your impact together will not be complete; it will be weak and less powerful.

Keep your love for God number one and then your love for one another. Honor and respect each other and watch your fruit be plenty!

*"As iron sharpens iron, So a man sharpens the countenance of his **friend**."*
-Proverbs 27:17 (NKJV)

Chapter Ten

Friends

Women seem to be designed to want close female "personal friends." This is healthy as long as proper boundaries are established early for everyone, including mate, family, and ministry. Sometimes being a pastor's wife can be a struggle in that area.

Every church seems to come equipped with people that strive to be just that, the "pastor's wife's friend". Especially if you are very outgoing and a people-person, you are setting yourself up to be a target. Generally everyone enjoys being around bubbly personalities and even though you are the wife of a pastor, you are not an exception. However, we must be wise in EVERY area of our walk.

I have always been a people-person and have at times struggled in that area because I love having friends and relationships in my life.

Early in our ministry I wanted to be just that, everybody's friend. I had this HUGE heart full of love and compassion for everyone that my cup *overfloweth*. However, *all this love*, created more problems than solutions due to others' own agendas and motives. Consequently, there were times I was left standing there, hurt and confused over relationships turned sour.

Wading through this long, up-to-my-neck season of battles and confrontations, we were also dealing with the sheep bites and bandages during this time. At which point, my husband and I ventured out to the mountains for a *"three day fast and seek God's direction for our lives"* weekend.

Do you see how awesome God is? Not only did I need healing from my sheep bites on that mountain, but He also gave me Rhema Word for my "friendships." (See Chapter 7.)

To reiterate, God clearly spoke to me and said, "I WILL GIVE YOU FRIENDS!" Those five Rhema words have proven to be a valuable tool for my *walk* unto this day. You are not delegated to be friends with everyone. Although you do have to be friendly; there is a difference between the two.

This released and relieved me at the same time. I was no longer responsible for being *everybody's friend.* Nevertheless, throughout the years, God has been faithful to His Word to bless me with some very wonderful friends! They have been loyal and genuine for many years!

"YOU, pastor's wife, along with God, must decide who you want to be that loyal friend."

I have learned through the *Bill Gothard* course that there are various levels of friendships.

I have two very special friends in particular! They have never placed demands on me but love me for who I am.

On one occasion, the Lord called my husband and me to pastor a church, where we remained there for seventeen years. One of my friends and her family came with us to this church, as we had been involved in a previous ministry commitment together. God sent her and her family there to support us.

God also sent another young lady during our season there, who came into my life and has remained not only a spiritual daughter, but a close friend as well. God knows just what we need in all seasons.

Together these special friends have walked me through some very difficult situations in my life. They have always been there when I needed them and would come today if I called. They are lifetime, God-sent friends.

Use wisdom in the "friends" area. Keep your "best friend" relationships low-key as you do not want to flaunt them in the presence of others. This does not mean to *not* associate with them whatsoever at Church, but just do not show "favorites" in the midst of others or you are setting yourself up for hurt. You will not be able to minister effectively if you are labeled to "pick and choose."

In order to *lead them all* you must remain on neutral ground with everyone.

In conclusion, **YES**, you *can* and *will* have some very close friends! They will be a Godsend to you. It is very important to establish proper boundaries early in relationships to allow them to flourish and survive.

God is faithful to everyone and does not want you to be alone. His Word says, "but there is a friend that sticks closer than a brother" (Prov. 18:24).

"Beloved, do not believe every spirit,
but test the spirits, whether they
are of God…"
-I John 4:1 (NKJV)

Chapter Eleven

Watch Out for "Jezze Belle"
(Feel free to read this chapter aloud to your husband, the pastor!)

There will be women in your congregation who have issues with fantasies. Can you believe that women have even had the nerve to tell me that they had a crush on my husband, and have actually dreamed that they were kissing him?

Oh please! The devil **is** *a liar!* I lie to you not.

Of course, I just laughed and pretty much wrote it off as being just plain 'ole stupid. But my comment to one was, "Yeah, well, thankfully, it was just a dream," as I laughed.

However, in this day and age you must guard against this thing. The "Jezebel spirit," or as I like to call her, "Jezze Belle," I believe is in every church. Women will view your husband as Prince Charming and as one who has the answer for everything. If a woman is not married

113

or has a rocky marriage, then *your husband* can become *her fantasy*.

Please do not be naïve and think that women will not attempt this, because trust me, **they will!** You have heard of these types of situations happening in churches all over the world. Your case will not be the first and it certainly will not be the last.

This is really not a laughing matter. Women, you see it on TV, soap operas, magazines, movies, etc. Jezze Belle has learned how to be very seductive. But remember, "no weapon formed against you shall prosper" (Isa 54:17). Praise God He gives us wisdom and understanding!

Encourage your husband to counsel women with the door open or with you present! Never shut the door! He may even have a secretary that sits in the office on the other side of the wall of his office, but I repeat, "DO NOT trust any woman with your husband, ever, any time, anywhere!" Wisdom, ladies, wisdom!

Sometimes, Pastor it may be wise to have your wife present during counseling. Be discerning!

Women who have a jezebel spirit are cunning and have one goal in mind - to bring your husband down to their level. She doesn't care about the ministry, she doesn't care about the church, she doesn't care about his reputation, and she certainly doesn't care about your or your family. Again, she has one goal in mind, and it is the only thing she wants, YOUR HUSBAND!

Miss Jezze will go after him at any cost. Lust begins to rage in her heart like a roaring lion and her prey often has no idea in the beginning. She draws near so innocently. Since men are very visual, she begins to scheme, plot and plan what her next move is going to be. She plays on his sympathy and sometimes her pity. If he has a compassionate heart, watch out! She begins to lure him into her grip that is like a vice and it isn't long before she wraps her emotions around his, and then pulls her victim under.

So you ask, "How can I help protect my mate?" First of all, love him, support him, meet his needs at home, affirm him, and praise him. If you have a concern, make him aware and discuss the "lioness" together openly. However, whatever you do, do not be a part of it and don't go along with what seems to be a joke. The enemy loves to take things like this and run with it. It is a chance for him to damage the Kingdom, whether the pastor's wife and lady friend are just joking about it or not. The enemy creates an opportunity for him, and if he can get an inch, he will take a mile.

Wives, I alert you to beware of Jezze Belle(s) in your church. But please do not view every woman as if her name is Jezze. Not all women have this intent in their heart. Just beware, be wise, stay sharp and keen. If you sense at any time someone is going after your husband, go to your husband first. If he does not listen, approach the proper authority and make every attempt to save your marriage and ministry.

God has brought you too far to let this spirit sneak in and cause destruction. Take it to the Master! For He will make your enemies your foot stool!

"Come to Me, all you who labor and are heavy laden, and I will give you rest."
-Matthew 11:28 (NKJV)

Chapter Twelve

Don't Be A People Pleaser

When we first moved into the church where we pastored for seventeen years, there was a woman who immediately wanted to befriend us. We had only been there a short time when one of the women's leaders approached me and said, "Watch out for so and so," she warned, "she will demand your friendship and manipulate your time. If you ever leave she won't have another thing to do with you." Truthfully, I didn't believe what I had heard.

As soon as we moved in our house, the woman began ringing our phone at 8am in the morning; as she was aware the pastor and I had set office hours. She would chat on the phone for several minutes and then offer to help out in any way possible.

The phone calls later converted to house calls at 8am. Since we had two small children, she assumed I would be home at that time. We did not have a garage, so if I was home, my car was parked in the yard. When she rang the doorbell, I had no other choice but to answer.

I discovered that she had lost her only son and her husband worked the day shift. In reality, she was lonely and did not want to be home alone during the day. At first, it wasn't so bad since I was new to the area and did not know anyone. But over a period of time, this began to seem like an annoyance rather than a blessing.

I tried everything to dodge her. I had a house to clean and would let her know, and her response would be, "I will help you, where's the mop?"

Though when I reflect back, she pretty much did anything I needed and helped me out tremendously.

She routinely cleaned our house, took care of the children, sacrificed revival services to care for our children during the school season, and picked them up after school if I was delayed at the office or out of town.

She and her husband became like grandparents to our sons. *That*, I didn't mind as I had lost both of my parents early in life; and living out of state we had no relatives within the area. I actually had prayed for people who would be like grandparents to our children and God had honored that prayer.

However, over a period of time this same woman became very jealous if other people came into my life. It was a very difficult situation that took us years to work through. It was apparent she could not accept me having additional friends and wanted to exit my life after eighteen years.

The right season finally came to discuss this situation with her, as I did not want to offend this lady, but she had put demands on our life. Eventually, I was able to bring clarity to our relationship by letting her know, "You are like a mom in my life." She accepted this "role," as my real mom had died around the time I was sixteen years old.

This put up proper boundaries, and I was able to form other relationships. All was well with everyone.

I share this story with you to shed some light by informing you that *you cannot please everyone*. It's impossible. While being a pastor's wife, it is very easy to want everyone to be your friend. You want to make everyone happy. But we must remember what the Lord said about this type of thing, "I DID NOT CALL YOU HERE TO BE THEIR FRIENDS, BUT I CALLED YOU HERE TO BE THEIR LEADER. I WILL GIVE YOU FRIENDS."

I can honestly say again, it's in our blood; we were designed to be accepted and loved. In our position, wanting to please everyone stems from the leader's desire to keep every soul that walks through the door satisfied as to grow the ministry.

The Word is clear that we are to reach out and love everyone. This can be done but again, you must set proper boundaries in place early on.

It is very important that people respect you in your position of authority. Regardless if they come to clean your house or hand you a tissue at the altar; keeping proper distance is essential. As your ministry grows to 250 and over, new boundaries will need to be re-established. Once you attain 500 and up, relationships will be redefined.

Let's take it to the Bible again. In Exodus 18 Moses shared all the victories won and all that the Lord had done, with his father-in-law, Jethro. Jethro thanked the Lord for all He had used Moses to accomplish. The next day Jethro came and asked Moses a few questions. "Why is all of this responsibility falling on you alone?" He said that this was not good. Jethro said to Moses to listen because he was going to give him some Godly counsel and advice. He said, "You must be the people's representative before God and bring their disputes to Him. Teach them the decrees and laws, and show them the way to live and the duties they are to perform. But select capable men from all the people – men who fear God, trustworthy men who hate dishonest gain – appoint them as officials over thousands, hundreds, fifties and tens. Have them serve as judges for the people at all times, but have them bring every difficult case to you; the simple cases they can decide themselves. That will make your load lighter, because they will share it with you. If you do this and God so commands, you will be able to stand the strain, and all these people will go home satisfied."

Moses listened to his father-in-law and did everything he said. He chose capable men from all of Israel and made them leaders of the people, officials over thousands, hundreds, fifties and tens. They served as judges for the people at all times. The difficult cases they brought to Moses, but the simple ones they decided themselves. (See Exodus 18.)

Pastors and their wives can spend so much time and energy on the complaints they hear that they find at times it is almost impossible to get to the important work. Delegation is so important. As Moses' father-in-law suggested, delegate most of the work to others and then you will be able to focus on the Word, the vision and direction for your ministry.

If you are so busy pleasing all the people, then you will be distracted and unable to do what God has called you to do effectively. You must de-clutter your *to-do* list of petty things.

Oftentimes you may feel like the only one who can do the job efficiently. God, however, has and will send you people to work along side of you that will be trustworthy, accountable, and efficient. Just as delegation relieved Moses of his stressful situations so that he could focus on what was at task for him to do, so will God provide for you. Just as God sent someone to help me when I needed it most, God will send help for you. Delegating to the people and giving them proper roles can relieve your responsibility and lighten your load. You will be able to accomplish much more as well as multiply in spiritual and numerical growth effectively.

Let your aim be that of pleasing the Father, not the people. If you please the Father, one day you will hear Him say to you, "Well done, good and faithful servant" (Matt. 25:21 NKJV).

"I press toward the goal for the prize of the upward call of God in Christ Jesus"
-Philippians 3:14 (NKJV)

Chapter Thirteen

Keep Your Eyes On The Prize

When people first come into the ministry they generally are filled with excitement and vision. They are eager and energetic to attack and accomplish the task that they know is deep seeded in their heart, soul, and mind. We all set out to run towards the goal, whatever that goal might be. Eagerly we run with zeal, motivated to accomplish the end result. We pursue with diligence, we put teams together with vigor. We work hard, day in and day out diligently pursuing the goal. As time goes on and the vision dims, we find ourselves weary, worn, and stressed out.

It is very easy to become distracted along the way. Distractions will come and may even come in the form of *good things*. It is ultimately important not to lose our focus.

We all remember and can relate to some, if not all of Nehemiah's story. He was a Man of

God who found people that had no wall around their city and who were left for prey and attack. He gathered the people together and began with a basic program. He helped care for the people and rallied around them to set up this program that would protect and be fair toward the people.

He established a sound government and not only did he begin to rebuild Jerusalem's walls, but with care he began to rebuild broken lives as well. He nurtured their spiritual needs.

Nehemiah was a very diligent and committed Man of God. His vision was to return to Jerusalem and bring the Jewish people back together and rebuild the walls that were broken down that represented shame. He knew that this would bring glory to God. His ultimate goal was to re-establish God's Presence and Power among the people.

He had so much compassion that he broke down and cried when he heard Jerusalem's walls were still in shambles and lying in rubble. Walls in Jerusalem were safety features. They represented peace inside of the walls and safety and strength on the outside. Nehemiah fasted and prayed for several days. He cried and poured his heart out to God and sought God regarding how he could help to repair the walls. He let God know how sorry he was for the sin the people had committed and it was his desire to see this totally restored.

Renewal and restoration often begins in the heart of one person. Nehemiah was no exception. In Chapter 2, verse 18 he shared his vision and they replied, "Let us rise up and build." Then they set their hands to this good work. (See Neh. 1, 2.)

Nehemiah worked diligently. He had a plan and a purpose and the support of the people. Just as we start our vision with diligence and vigor, Nehemiah did likewise.

Early in the chapter we mentioned that distractions would come. They are mere stepping stones. When you come to one it can feel like it has been sent to trip you up and wants to cause you to trip, stumble and fall.

First, the enemy does not want a good work to progress so he may try to interrupt or interfere. We know that he has no power to stay and we usually jump this first hurtle. When the obstacles start coming at a rapid rate, we may trip, we my stagger, but we get up again and again and again. *Now we're learning to roll with the punches, you see!*

We know that Isaiah 54:17 says, "No weapon formed against you shall prosper" (NKJV).

Nehemiah started having problems with the Jews who were loaning money and charging those who were in need with high interest rates. So Nehemiah addressed the issue. Then the attacks came on Nehemiah's character. Rumors started to fly along with false reports. *Sound familiar?*

This often happens to leaders and can be disappointing and even greatly devastating.

Many times attacks come from people that you love and pour yourself into, making it even all the more hurtful. When you are doing God's work you can expect this to happen, because people are people *everywhere.* Ecclesiastes 1:9 says, "There is no new thing under the sun."

Know that when you are doing God's work, you may receive several attacks on your character. Do as Nehemiah did and trust God to make you strong under the attack, and do not return to get vengeance for, "Vengeance is mine, I will repay, says the Lord" (Rom. 12:19, NKJV).

Know that there will be the "Sanballats" along the way. If you expect it, then you will not be surprised when they come. These people have a knack for stirring up trouble; they may even try to turn your people against you. Sanballat's accusations were not true, and since Nehemiah knew they were not true, he just kept right on going. *What a motivating story! Praise God that he refused to be diverted from the goal.*

You never measure yourself next to another leader. God's Word is your measure. We must constantly check our behavior with God's standards in His Word. We have to guard our hearts from falling back into old patterns and old ways. Nehemiah overcame great obstacles and we can too. We should all learn from our mistakes to avoid repeating them in the future. If you look over your mistakes and things of your past, it will keep you in line and divine order so that the Blessings of God can flow.

Keep your eyes on the prize which is Christ Jesus. Do not divert to the left or right, but keep focused on what God has called you to do. Do not quit, do not even entertain the possibility. God is a Big God, and what He has called you to do, He will finish just as He did with Nehemiah. Again I declare, keep your eyes on the prize and run the race! When you have completed it, you will receive your reward.

Though there are situations and many hats that can be very stressful at times in the ministry, there are also many good times as well. But we are not called in the ministry to just have a good time. God has entrusted us with teaching Kingdom principles in people's lives. We all will stand before God one day and give an account for all that He has entrusted us to accomplish in our lifetime. It is about seeing souls saved and lives changed. It is about making disciples to further His Kingdom. It is such an honor to serve our King. Always remember, "And let us not grow weary while doing good, for in due season we shall reap if we do not lose heart" (Gal. 6:9 NKJV).

I pray this book has been an encouragement to you and informed you that you are certainly not alone in this race. We are in this together, and God is counting on us to complete the work that He has given us. **We are never alone!**

"He who calls you is faithful, who also will do it" (I Th. 5:24, NKJV).

LaVergne, TN USA
04 February 2010
172063LV00001B/1/P

9 781615 796182